D1569568

Virginia Wingo:
Teacher and Friend

BARBARA MASSEY

Illustrated by Jack Woodson

932

BROADMAN PRESS
Nashville, Tennessee

First Baptist Church
MEDIA LIBRARY

To
Virginia Wingo,
the missionary I remember
first praying for as a member of GA

© Copyright 1983 • Broadman Press
All rights reserved.
ISBN: 0-8054-4282-0
4242-82

Dewey Decimal Classification: J266.092
Subject headings: WINGO, VIRGINIA / / MISSIONS—ITALY
Library of Congress Catalog Card Number: 82-073665
Printed in the United States of America

Contents

Brother and Friend

"Virginia," Mrs. Wingo called to her daughter. "You come and play in the backyard. And, Spurgeon, you go to the front yard to play. You must play alone until you can learn to get along."

The Wingos lived in Slidell, Louisiana. Mr. Wingo was the pastor of the Slidell Baptist Church. The house right next to the church was their home. The yard was very large. It was divided into a front yard and a backyard by a picket fence. The fence did not have a gate.

Sometimes Virginia and Brother, as she called him, fussed with each other. Mrs. Wingo would separate them. One would go to the backyard to play. The other would go to the front. But they very quickly learned how to get back together.

"Sis," called Brother from the front yard. "Let's play a game." It would not be long until they were happily playing a game together. They could play through the fence!

Working out problems like this made Virginia and Brother very special friends.

4

School Days

Brother started to school first. Virginia had to stay at home. She was not old enough to go to first grade. But something exciting happened that year.

Virginia had a very special teacher. Her mother! She had a very special school. Her home! Mrs. Wingo was a good teacher. And she had a very good student. But they both had help. Every day Brother came home from school and told Virginia what he had learned. Then Mother would go over the lessons with both of them. Virginia and Brother learned together. Virginia worked hard on her school work. She wanted to keep up with Brother.

The next year the teacher said, "You are ready for second grade, Virginia." So Brother and Virginia began second grade together.

Another important thing happened to Virginia the next year. This was more important than skipping first grade.

Growing up in a preacher's home, she had

always gone to church. She had always heard
about Jesus. She listened to her father preach.
She learned to follow the Bible reading. She
understood much of what he said in his sermons.
He told lots of stories. Virginia loved them.

She began to realize that Jesus was more than
someone she heard about at home and church.
She knew that she wanted to become a follower
of Jesus.

When Virginia was seven years old, she
became a Christian. How special it was to have
her own father baptize her.

Growing Up

Virginia Wingo was the only daughter in her family. Brother was the only son. He was only fourteen months older than Virginia. But he was always her "big" brother. She always said that her parents gave her a great gift. That gift was a big brother.

Virginia grew up in Slidell and Bogalusa, Louisiana. And she really grew *up*. Virginia was always taller than her friends. Sometimes being tall made her feel timid and shy. She grew to be six-feet tall as an adult.

Virginia never really liked school. But reading was different. It was fun. Often she won first or second place in spelling matches. She saved the little blue and pink ribbons given to her.

More than anything Virginia loved vacation. Summer days were filled with plenty of friends to play with. They enjoyed playing ball, climbing trees, roller skating, swimming, and hiking.

Doing things together was fun for the Wingo family.

"You read to us tonight, Sister," Papa often said. The family enjoyed reading aloud.

Singing together was also a special time. The whole family enjoyed singing hymns. Sometimes ten-year-old Virginia played the piano for them. She had taken a few piano lessons. And she liked to play hymns for the family.

Virginia loved to sing. Once she even won a prize for singing. It was during a revival meeting at her church.

"I have a prize," said the choir director. "I'll give twenty-five cents to the child who will sing the loudest in church today."

"A quarter," thought Virginia. "I can win that." And she did.

The Young Disciples

"Sis," called Brother one day. "I've got an idea. I need your help."

"OK," said Virginia. Brother always had good ideas.

"Let's start a club," he suggested.

"What kind of club?" asked Virginia. She was interested in the idea.

"Well," said Brother. "I want it to be a club for helping people. We could even do jobs at the church. Maybe we could wash windows."

"Let's do it," said Virginia. She was excited. "That's a great idea. When do we meet? Where will the meeting be?"

"I thought about meeting at church once a week," answered Brother. "Right after school."

"Our club needs a name," he said. "I can't think of a good one. Have you got any ideas?"

"How about the Young Disciples?" offered Virginia. "That sounds like a good name."

Brother and Virginia quickly began to talk to their friends. They needed club members.

Even when she was very young, Virginia Wingo enjoyed helping others. She wanted to be a friend to others.

An Important Decision

"What an exciting place," thought Virginia. She listened as a missionary spoke in her church.

Many times Virginia heard about faraway places. Her father often asked missionaries to speak at church. The missionaries told about the countries where they worked. Virginia listened carefully. She learned about people and their needs. Maybe one day she, too, could go help.

Virginia read a book about a missionary. She became very interested in missions. The book was the story of a missionary who worked with lepers in India. Virginia's interest grew. She read about missionaries William Carey and David Livingstone. Their lives seemed exciting. Their work seemed important.

Virginia went to camp when she was fourteen. She listened as the speakers talked about missions. During this time, she began to feel that God wanted her to do something special for him. She began to feel that God wanted her to be a foreign missionary one day.

Virginia returned home from camp. She decided to read the Bible straight through every year. The first time she read quickly. She read the whole Bible in twenty-five days.

First Baptist Church
MEDIA LIBRARY

Going to the Fair

"Today is the day Mary and I go to the fair," Virginia said to herself. She put on the beautiful, new, blue dress that Mother had made for her.

As Virginia started out the door, Mother called, "Sister, don't forget your hat."

"Oh, no," grumbled Virginia to herself. She did not like hats at all. But she put the hat on.

She walked to Mary's house. Mary was not wearing a hat. "I'll leave my hat here. I'll get it on the way home," Virginia told Mary.

That afternoon, Virginia picked up her hat at Mary's. Carefully she placed it on her head. She didn't know that the wind had blown her hair. Then she walked home.

"Hello, Sister," Mother called to her. "Did you have fun at the fair?" Then Mother saw Virginia's hair. "You didn't wear your hat, did you?"

"No," answered Virginia sadly. "It's always easy to disobey," she thought. "But it makes me feel unhappy to do it."

14

A Promise Kept

Virginia and Brother graduated from high school. Then the Wingo family moved to Pineville, Louisiana. There Virginia and Brother went to Louisiana College.

Virginia became a teacher. She liked teaching. But she still felt there was something else she should do. What that something else was, she was not sure.

Soon she began to find out. A trip to a camp in North Carolina helped her know. She talked to friends and leaders there.

"I've got a good job now," thought Virginia. "Why should I leave it? But I've been offered a scholarship to the training school in Louisville two times. I've turned it down. Besides, what will the training school prepare me for anyway? Foreign missions?"

Virginia began to pray. "Lord," she said. "Do you want me to go to the training school? If so, let the scholarship be offered again. I promise to accept it."

Before long, the scholarship was offered
again. Just as she had promised, Virginia
accepted. Soon she was a student at the training
school.

Even in Louisiana

Virginia had an important decision to make. "I need to talk to the Lord about this," she thought.

There was a special room at the training school. It was called the Lottie Moon Prayer Room. Virginia had not been there many times. But one day she went there. She needed some time to think and to pray. She went in. She locked the door.

"I will go to Africa," she said. "I will go to China. I will go anywhere else the Lord wants me to go. But there is one place I do not want to go. I do not want to work in Louisiana."

Before Virginia left the prayer room, she was able to say: "Lord, I will work anywhere. If you want, I will work even in Louisiana."

School ended that year. Virginia packed to go home. She was happy about her decision.

"I'll be back next year," she thought.

While Virginia was home, a letter came to her. The letter said:

DEAR VIRGINIA:

We want you to come to work for us. We want you to help with the missions organizations for children. Would you do this instead of going back to school?

Sincerely,

MISS HANNAH REYNOLDS, Executive Director

Woman's Missionary Union of Louisiana

Virginia was surprised! But she remembered what had happened that day in the prayer room. She remembered that she had promised: "I will work anywhere. I will work even in Louisiana."

Virginia began her work in Louisiana. She was happy with her job. She could not believe that she was being paid to do it.

A Teacher Again

DEAR VIRGINIA:

We would like for you to think about coming back to Louisville. We want to invite you to be a teacher. We want you to teach missionary education in the training school.

> Sincerely,
> DR. CARRIE LITTLEJOHN,
> President
> Woman's Missionary Union
> Training School

Virginia wanted to stay in Louisiana. But she knew the answer to the letter must be yes.

She went to the training school and began teaching classes. She told her students: "God hasn't called me to be a foreign missionary yet. If he had, I would have gone."

Just a few days later, Virginia heard a missionary from Brazil speak. She listened to Alberta Steward tell about her work at the Woman's Missionary Union Training School in Recife, Brazil. This helped Virginia know that

God wanted her to be a foreign missionary. She wrote a letter to the Foreign Mission Board. She felt she might be used as a teacher in Brazil.

One day Virginia had a special visitor. Her name was Mrs. Martin. She brought Virginia an interesting message.

"Dr. Rankin from the Foreign Mission Board and I have chosen and bought some property in Rome, Italy," she said. "We are planning to build a Christian training school. This school will be for Italian young women.

"We need a director for this school," she said. "We did not know you were interested in foreign missions. Then the Foreign Mission Board got your letter asking about the school in Brazil."

Virginia made a trip to Richmond, Virginia. She visited with Dr. Rankin at the Foreign Mission Board.

On a wall in Dr. Rankin's office, Virginia saw a map of the world. She saw Italy. It was the shape of a boot. She and Dr. Rankin talked about missions in Italy. Virginia looked at the map. She saw Italy more than any other place. Virginia was sure now that Rome was the place. That was where God wanted her to serve as a foreign missionary.

A New Country

Virginia was busy the next few weeks. She had to get ready to leave for Italy. She went to Louisiana to visit her family. It would be a long time before she saw them again. And she had to pack all of her things.

Finally, the day came for Virginia to leave for Italy. She left New York on the ship *Saturnia*. As she sailed, she thought about her family at home. "I will miss them." She thought about her new country. "What will the people be like? Will I ever learn their language?"

In Italy she was met by other missionaries. They made her feel like part of their families.

In Rome, she saw the Armstrong Memorial Training School being built. The second floor had been started. Soon there would be three floors. The school was being built on a low hill near a river.

"How beautiful," Virginia smiled as she looked at the land. Between the school and the river she saw a large pasture for sheep. She saw

wheat fields. They would be golden with wheat by next summer. How she looked forward to the day the school would be open!

Money to build the school was sent by many churches in the United States. Finally, it was completed. Italian girls would live and study there.

The first four students arrived soon. Virginia moved into her apartment at the school. There was much excitement! Dedication Day was planned. There was much to do.

"We need to make curtains and tablecloths," Virginia told the students.

What a wonderful time they had together. On the first morning, the five new friends had a

24

worship service together.

The girls did not pay to go to the school or to live there. They did not pay for food. They all had jobs at the school. Some cleaned. Some washed dishes. This helped pay for their education.

"The way we work together" one of the girls said, "makes this seem like a family. It's like school, home, and church here."

Virginia had begun her long friendship with the Italian people. They learned that she had come to live in their country. She had not just come for a little while.

"Why have you come to live here," they would ask her. Then Virginia would tell them about Jesus.

For twenty years Virginia Wingo was the director of the Armstrong Memorial Training School. She taught English to the Italian students. The school was called *Istituto Betania* by the Italians.

Virginia was a friend to all the students. She was a friend to their families.

Something New

"I don't think I'll ever be as happy in Rivoli as I am in Rome," thought Virginia.

Fewer and fewer students were coming to the Armstrong Memorial Training School. Students were attending other schools in Italy. So the training school closed.

Soon Virginia moved to Rivoli to work in another school. It was called Philadelphia Center.

"Thank you, Lord. Thank you," said Virginia out loud. She walked across the campus on her first night there. It already seemed like home to her. Her work at the training school had prepared her for this new work.

"I'm going to be happy here," she thought.

I'll Stay

Many years went by. It was almost time for Virginia to retire. She planned to move back to America.

"Why are you going back to America?" a visitor to Philadelphia Center asked Virginia one day.

Virginia began to think about what her visitor had said.

"Why should I go back to America and just talk about missions in Italy?" she asked herself. "I still might be able to help here."

She talked to some friends. "We think it is a good idea for you to stay," they told her.

In 1978, Virginia began another exciting part of her life. "We need you here," an Italian pastor told her. "I have been praying for someone to help me in the church," he said.

"I'll stay," Virginia happily told him.

Virginia Wingo continues to love the Italian people. They love her. They are happy when they see their tall friend with the snow-white hair and the smiling face.

Virginia likes living in Italy. She enjoys being a teacher and friend to the Italian people.

GERMANY
SWITZERLAND
AUSTRIA
RIVOLI
VENICE
ITALY
YUGOSLAVIA
FLORENCE
ROME
MEDITERRANEAN SEA

Remember

Virginia Wingo learned early to be a friend to others. She was a good friend to members of her family. Her family liked doing things together.

What are some things they did?

How can you be a good friend to your family?

As a child, Virginia learned about faraway countries. She learned about people who lived there.

What are some ways she learned about missions?

How can you learn about missions?

Ask your pastor or a teacher to invite a missionary to speak in your church.

Virginia listened to missionaries speak in her church when she was a child. She listened to speakers at camp. She talked with friends and teachers who were interested in her.

How do you think God helped Virginia know what he wanted her to do?

About the Author

If you lived in my neighborhood, you would see me jogging and riding my ten-speed bicycle a lot. You might even come bake chocolate chip cookies with me. That's what the children in my neighborhood do.

Hi! My name is Barbara Massey, and I live in Birmingham, Alabama.

My job is fun. I am the editor of two magazines. One of them, *Aware*, is a magazine for teachers. *Discovery* is a magazine that helps girls in grades one through six learn about missions. The place where I work is Woman's Missionary Union.

The children in my church are special friends. I am one of their teachers. I enjoy being with children and being their teacher and friend.

BROADMAN